SandCastle™

Giant Animals

GIRAFFE

ANDERS HANSON

Consulting Editor, Diane Craig, M.A./Reading Specialist

A Division of ABDO

ABDO
Publishing Company

visit us at www.abdopublishing.com

Published by ABDO Publishing Company, a division of ABDO, P.O. Box 398166, Minneapolis, Minnesota 55439. Copyright © 2014 by Abdo Consulting Group, Inc. International copyrights reserved in all countries. No part of this book may be reproduced in any form without written permission from the publisher. SandCastle™ is a trademark and logo of ABDO Publishing Company.

Printed in the United States of America, North Mankato, Minnesota
102013
012014

 PRINTED ON RECYCLED PAPER

Editor: Liz Salzmann
Content Developer: Nancy Tuminelly
Cover and Interior Design and Production: Anders Hanson, Mighty Media, Inc.
Photo Credits: Shutterstock, Thinkstock

Library of Congress Cataloging-in-Publication Data
Hanson, Anders, 1980- author.
  Giraffe / Anders Hanson ; consulting editor, Diane Craig, M.A., reading specialist.
     pages cm. -- (Giant animals)
  Audience: 4 to 9.
  ISBN 978-1-62403-058-1
1. Giraffe--Juvenile literature. I. Craig, Diane, editor. II. Title.
  QL737.U56H36 2014
  599.638--dc23
                          2013023935

SandCastle™ Level: Transitional

SandCastle™ books are created by a team of professional educators, reading specialists, and content developers around five essential components—phonemic awareness, phonics, vocabulary, text comprehension, and fluency—to assist young readers as they develop reading skills and strategies and increase their general knowledge. All books are written, reviewed, and leveled for guided reading, early reading intervention, and Accelerated Reader® programs for use in shared, guided, and independent reading and writing activities to support a balanced approach to literacy instruction. The SandCastle™ series has four levels that correspond to early literacy development. The levels are provided to help teachers and parents select appropriate books for young readers.

Emerging Readers (no flags)   Beginning Readers (1 flag)   Transitional Readers (2 flags)   Fluent Readers (3 flags)

contents

HELLO, GIRAFFE!

Giraffes are **mammals** with very long necks. They live in Africa. They are the tallest land animals. Giraffes grow up to 20 feet (6 m) tall!

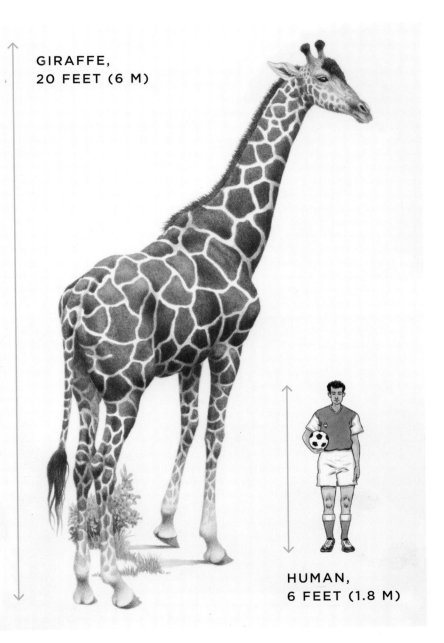

GIRAFFE,
20 FEET (6 M)

HUMAN,
6 FEET (1.8 M)

WHAT A NECK!

Giraffes have the longest necks. Their necks can be up to 6 feet (1.8 m) long!

WHAT DO YOU EAT?

Giraffes eat mostly leaves and **twigs**. Giraffes use their necks to reach food high in the trees.

COOL SPOTS!

A giraffe's coat has brown spots. The spots are **separated** by white lines. Every giraffe's spots are different.

ARE THOSE HORNS?

Giraffes have two **knobs** on top of their heads. They are made of **cartilage**. This means they are not horns. Horns are made of bone.

WEIRD TONGUE!

Giraffes have purple **tongues**. They're 20 inches (50 cm) long! Giraffes pull leaves off trees with their tongues. They also lick their noses. Yuck!

WHERE ARE YOU GOING?

Giraffes can run fast. They can reach 37 miles per hour (60 km/h)!

WHERE DO YOU LIVE?

Giraffes live in Africa. They are found where there is grass and trees. Giraffes don't need much water.

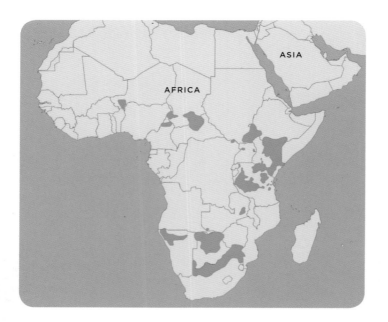

DO YOU HAVE A FAMILY?

A baby giraffe is called a calf.
A calf is 6 feet (1.8 m) tall when
it is born. A mother giraffe has
one calf at a time.

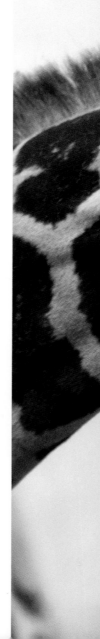

QUICK QUIZ

Check your answers below!

1. **Giraffes are the tallest land animals.** TRUE OR FALSE?

2. **All giraffes' spots look the same.** TRUE OR FALSE?

3. **Giraffes can lick their noses.** TRUE OR FALSE?

4. **Giraffes can run fast.** TRUE OR FALSE?

1) True 2) False 3) True 4) True

GLOSSARY

cartilage – a strong, elastic tissue that makes up some parts of humans and other mammals, such as ears, noses, and joints.

knob – a round lump.

mammal – a warm-blooded animal that has hair and whose females produce milk to feed their young.

separated – divided or kept apart.

tongue – the movable muscle in the mouth that is used for tasting and swallowing.

twig – a thin, small branch of a tree or a bush.